LAST POEMS

Paul Celan

Translated by Katharine Washburn
and Margret Guillemin

NORTH POINT PRESS *San Francisco*

Conversation in the Mountains first appeared in *The Paris
Review* in 1981, to which grateful acknowledgment is
made.

Quotations from Michael Hamburger and from his
translations of poems by Paul Celan are used with
permission of Michael Hamburger and with the
permission of the publishers of his book, *Celan: Poems*,
published in 1980 by Persea Books in New York and
Carcanet Press in Manchester, England.

Printed in the United States of America
Library of Congress Catalogue Card Number: 85-72978
ISBN: 0-86547-224-6

North Point Press
850 Talbot Avenue
Berkeley, California
94706

INTRODUCTION

I

The man who cries out with pain, or says he has pain, doesn't choose the mouth which says it.

    L. WITTGENSTEIN, *The Blue and Brown Books*

We are digging the pit of Babel.

    KAFKA

Paul Ancel was born in Czernowitz, the capital of Romanian Bukovina, in November, 1920. Growing up as the son of Jewish parents in a German-speaking milieu, he acquired a multiplicity of tongues: Hebrew as part of the religious education required by an Orthodox parent, Romanian through local schooling, a fluency in French expanded through a year of medical school in Tours, in 1938, and a program of study in Romance philology after his return to Romania the following summer. It is possible that the son's academic ambitions served to postpone the Zionist father's plan of emigration to Palestine. In any event, the Ancel family continued to live in Czernowitz under the German occupation until the deportation of the parents in June of 1942. In the autumn of that year they were shot by the S.S. Their son survived to become the

German-language poet Paul Celan and to encompass their deaths in poem after poem in which autumn, ever the season of elegy, becomes a cipher for catastrophic loss. The writer Celan, who insisted, after all, in an inscription scrawled to his most eminent English translator, Michael Hamburger, that he was *"ganz und gar nicht hermetisch,"* absolutely not hermetic, recalls their murder in a line from an early poem utterly emblematic of the power the murderer's language could release for him:

> . . . du starbst nicht
> den malvenfarbenen Tod.

You didn't die the mauve death: The reader who gives Celan's verse the long scrutiny he recommended finds encased in those elegant syllables, addressed to his dead mother, not only the elliptical reference to death by asphyxiation in the gas chamber, but an allusion, in the German compound in which Celan plants his metaphor, to I. G. Farben, the manufacturer of cyanide. (The above is an example of the novice poet's talent for invective underscored by double entendre, one which will invade and sometimes dominate the field of his later work.)*

Factual details of this poet's wartime history, already confused and sketchy, are further blurred by the shuffle in Ro-

---

*The very name *Ancel* will dwindle into poetic cipher, a sough of syllables in the late poems. George Steiner has located such a reverberation in the *Amselpaar* of "Largo," a poem excluded from this collection. The reader here might consider instead: "the one- / winged soaring blackbird, / above the firewall, behind / Paris, up there. . . ." Celan celebrates a glimpse, during the riots of 1968, of the black flag of anarchism and fuses it with the sound of his original name.

mania of two successive occupying powers: Germany and the Soviet Union. It is known* that Paul Ancel was first set to work hauling debris from the Prut River. Later he was sent to shovel rocks on the roads in southeast Romania: Perhaps the most coherent narrative of those years lies in his poetry, in the constellation of images organized around debris, barges, stone, rock, darkness, snow, and minerals. Little else is known, although a story published in a German newspaper in the late seventies proposes that Ancel was haunted by the memory of escaping execution in the detention camp by "jumping the line," sliding from his designated place in a formation bound for the trucks and the bullets into the place of a man bound for the uncertain fate of hard labor. As Primo Levi's memoir of Auschwitz observes that every man's survival, in such extremity, depended on another man's extinction, one may find the prominence given this account somewhat dubious. After the war, orphaned by the German occupation and dispossessed by the Soviet, the survivor left Bucharest in 1947 with a rucksack of poems. Following a six-month sojourn in Vienna, he emigrated to Paris where he lived for a quarter of a century "after the first death" as Paul Celan.

The pseudonym, contrived in Bucharest, and sealed in Vienna, from an anagram of the original name, dissolved its ambiguous cultural identity into a number of allusions to the primary concerns of his poetry. Paul Celan, amateur botanist and poet of the eye, most likely knew the reputation of the herb *celandine* for curing weak sight. The former student of

*I am indebted here, not for the last time, to the researches of Jerry Glenn and John Felstiner.

fourteenth-century Romance philology, who had a particular attachment to the canticles of Francis of Assisi, must have relished the echo of the name of the author of the *Dies Irae*, Thomas of Celano. We are accustomed, in the poems, to Celan's habit of breaking down a given word, exhausting it etymologically and supplying it with the densest and widest repetoire of associations. In the name itself, we have the writer's shortest poem, composed at the edge of known languages.

The decision to write poetry in German, however, raises all those questions of nationality and culture which an ambiguous surname rebuffs. Paul Celan came from a province washed by the rivers of at least four languages: Romanian, Yiddish, German, and Russian. His education in French and Hebrew increased their number to six. Bukovinia, now split between Romania and the USSR, had been part of the Austro-Hungarian Empire, and the Jewish settlement there, according to social stratum, spoke Yiddish or German. Celan was schooled in German humanistic culture, and his close attachment to his German-speaking mother, the dead woman whose soul "helps to navigate night, reef after reef," suggests the primacy of German as the language for the inner life. The same poem tells us explicitly that "This word is your mother's ward. . . . Your mother's ward stoops for the crumb of light." The biographer of his early years, Israel Chalfen, records Celan's own gloss on this matter: "Only in one's mother tongue can one express one's own truth. In a foreign language the poet lies." Unbearably, the word is German.

Although Celan did publish some very early poems in Romanian, that language was evidently too thin, too external a medium for him. As a writer whose gaze was turned west, he accepted an endowment from Russian of a receptive order—as translator of Blok, Essenin, and most significantly for his own development, Osip Mandelstam. Despite his profound debt to the work of the French surrealists, Michaux, Eluard, and the Franco-German Goll, and his permanent residence in France, Celan was clearly compelled to write in German, a language of long shadows. Like the traveller fluent in many languages, caught in a moment of great pain or emotional intensity, who breaks into his native tongue, this poet, whose final poems summon again and again the images of severed tongues, fingers lopped from the (writing) hand, and mouths choked with earth or sealed against speech, required the slow richness and long deprivation of linguistic exile. He spent his life in Paris as teacher, translator, and poet in a linguistic coccoon, spinning poems from a language nourished chiefly by the letter and cut off at the source. The result of this series of literary and cultural transformations was the creation of an anomalous German language, reclaimed from the darkness yet capable of addressing it.

The reader of Celan's poetry is spared little of the self-destructive character of this pact with the German tongue, a language he himself described as having to "pass through its own unresponsiveness, pass through its own fearful muting, pass through the thousand darknesses of death-bringing speech." We feel the solitude of this long dialogue with the German dictionary, the atomization of a poetic vocabulary, the suppression of the lyric ego—and tally them in the grave expense of the redemptive task. The heir of Hölderlin and Rilke undertook a lustration of their language which almost wore it away. Most of us would confirm George Steiner's judgment that in the end, Paul Celan is writing German *like a foreign language*.

Celan described the trajectory of his own poetic career as "still geworden," becoming silent. The course of his personal life seems to have been marked by great psychic distress, turmoil, and breakdown. A visitor observing him in company a number of times in the last five years of his life recalls a dark and isolated presence, a man who sat alone immersed in geology texts. The immense difficulties of his last poems, which refract and draw from the antediluvian landscapes of those same geology books, the rising dissonance and fierce compression of his work in the last decade of his life, and the troubled character of that life, which ended with suicide by drowning in the Seine in April, 1970, have all contributed to the legend of the Celan of the ultimate *expressivo* stammer, the musician of the Holocaust struck dumb by terror and anxiety, who ends by making a burnt offering of language itself.

But there is another reading, more affirmative, of that poetic development whose beginning was announced by the publication of his first volume of poetry, *Sand from the Urns* in Vienna, in 1948. The author, apparently appalled by a proliferation of misprints in the first edition, withdrew this book from further printings, retaining twenty poems from this early volume for inclusion in *Mohn und Gedächnis, Poppy and Memory*. The title of this book pointed with a fine vividness to the central predicament of Celan's poetry—the unstable and dangerous union between Paul Celan, caught early in that sensual music of the Surrealists, pure poet of the intoxicating line, and Paul Ancel, heir and hostage to the most lacerating of human memories. A line from a late poem, included among the translations in the present volume, describes this tension:

> I drink wine
> from two glasses . . .

"Like *that one*, with Pindar." (*That one* is no doubt Hölderlin, a poet on the threshold between delusion and prophecy, who, as Michael Hamburger has observed, anticipated the exploration of "positive irrationality" by one hundred and fifty years while his contemporary audience slowly ebbed away.) Its temporary resolution in *Mohn und Gedächnis*, published in Germany in 1952, won him wide critical acclaim, an invitation to Group 47 under the chairmanship of Hans Werner Richter, and a firm place in the most enduring succession in German literature: The poetic tradition of dithyrambic invention which stretches from Hölderlin through Trakl and Rilke. What was launched, however, in those early years, on that tide of exuberant lyricism, was not only the reputation of the greatest of post-war German poets, but the first wave of Celan's "light-words." The early volumes spill almost every letter of Celan's private alphabet. They establish a vocabulary that will not only remain intact through every metamorphosis, new accretions, new pairings and uncouplings, through book after book of Celan's work, but a linguistic genesis in which everything—the authenticity and accessibility of the poem—will depend on their utter integrity.

A new poetic lexicon displays its pivot-words, words Celan later called "primers of pulse-sound." They are all here, the elements for a language that will gradually cease to explain itself: hair, sand, eyes, stone, star, leaf, autumn, flower, boat, mouth, rain, snow, ring. This list comprises a portion of the nouns, yet only a close reading of Celan's entire work will begin to reveal the depth of their relation with each other—the highly wrought grid of language in which a hurled stone becomes a star, a boat is a coffin and a bed, rain alternates with snow, tears become rain, rain turns to tears and tears to steam, rain is a sign of God's grace, and once more, rain is transmuted into "snow-summered over," while snow unites with bed to become a snow-bed in the realm of the dead. The verbs will include digging, counting, wearing, bearing, drinking, opening, reading, growing, in a multiplicity of conjunctions with the nouns, which will continue, with the special faculty granted to them by the morphology of German grammar, to form dyads with other nouns, couple with adverbial endings, and mutate into verbs, so that things *grow* autumnwards, hair shares the attributes of a leaf, the leaf falls at once from book, tree, or calendar. Henceforth, a language merges with such a dense, allusive, and sinewy connective tissue that after accustomizing ourselves to the features of this landscape, we can read a line such as

> A star-
> porous leaf
> for a mouth,

and respond with some gesture of recognition. The leaf penetrated by light, in Celan's concordance of meaning, may be a poem. A poetic utterance displaces a mouth—that is, ordinary speech.

The translator of Celan benefits from his advice to Chalfen throughout the extended labor of the task: The process of translating a poem requires that one ". . . Read! Just read again and again, the understanding comes by itself." One learns indeed to puzzle out, over many readings, the personal, historical, and literary data, the strands of associations, obsessions, and allusions which fuse in a single poem, and to be content, finally, with a sympathetic unknowing—the state of readership in which some genuine perception may at last become possible. We have no miraculous codex, no Rosetta Stone, for a language not so much lost as still to be written. Perhaps the most potent injunction is within an early poem:

> With a variable key
> you unlock the house in which
> drifts the snow of that left unspoken
> Always what key you choose
> Depends on the blood that spurts
> from your eye or your mouth or your ear . . .

The poem is a house or a *techné*. (The snow-bound house will reappear in *Schneepart*, this time "forever windowless.") The thing made is open to entry, but must remain forever open to the unsaid, the drift of snow. It is the tenancy of silence, erected to lie open to what cannot be given human utterance:

> You vary the key,
> you vary the word
> that is free to drift with the flakes.
> What snowball will form round the word
> depends on the wind that rebuffs you.
> (TR. MICHAEL HAMBURGER)

Urged toward such understanding, we are forced to abide the most tentative and partial solution. Thus, it is possible to say of the longer, earlier "Chanson einer Dame im Schatten," "Chanson of a Lady in the Shade," that under the elegant dandyesque refrain of the poem, with its echoes of Rimbaud and Goll, its elements of sapphire and lust, is some trace of the dark deposit of guilt and despair in many of these poems, the narrative baggage carried everywhere and never thrown away.

> When the silent one comes and beheads the tulips:
> Who wins?
>   Who loses?
>   Who walks to the window?
> Who's the first to speak her name?
>
> He is one who wears my hair.
> He wears it much as one wears the dead on one's hands,
> He wears it much as the sky wore my hair that year
>   when I loved.
> He wears it like that out of vanity.
>
> That one wins.
>   Doesn't lose.
>   Doesn't walk to the window.
> He does not speak her name.
>
> He is one who has my eyes.
> He's had them since gates have shut.
> He wears them like rings on his fingers.
> He wears them like shards of sapphire and lust;
> Since the autumn he has been my brother;
> He's counting the days and the nights.

That one wins.
　　Doesn't lose.
　　　　Doesn't walk to the window.
He's the last to speak her name.

He's one who has what I said.
He carries it under his arm like a bundle.
He carries it as the clock carries its worst hour.
From threshold to threshold he carries it, never throws it away.

That one doesn't win.
　　He loses.
　　　　He walks to the window.
He's the first to speak her name.

With tulips that one's beheaded.
(TR. MICHAEL HAMBURGER)

The title reflects the hybrid character of this youthful poem: "Chanson einer Dame im Schatten." The playful, erotic properties of a Gallic form are crossed with something darker. A French surrealist troubadour is speaking German. Under the melodic, almost lush surface of the poem, one finds an encoded fragment of Celan's painful history and the words he selected not only to give it utterance but to preserve the silence and secrecy which must be rendered to sacred things. The invisible autarch of the Celan's poetry is silence: He is bound by Mallarmé's warning that "Whatever is sacred, whatever is to *remain* sacred, must be clothed in mystery."

The season is autumn, and the gates whose opening is sought in one of the last prayers on Yom Kippur are shut. The sacred element of this poem is the death of Celan's mother, the one of whom he doesn't speak, whose lost hair is turned to smoke: that is, worn by the sky. (*But: "He wears it like that out of vanity"—he celebrates it to make poems.*)* Sky and hair converge in the next refrain as "shards of sapphire and lust," worn like rings on the fingers as a compact with the dead. To have the "eyes of the dead," to go on seeing the universe through their eyes, requires the discipline of silence and indirection, relieved only by the life of the poem—the walk to the window for a breath of air. Walking, like breathing, in Celan, is among other things a precise symbol for metrical speech: The creation of the poem.

The "he" of the poem is one of Celan's unstable particles. His pronouns shift gender, address the male and female aspects of the poet, invoke the masculine and feminine aspects of God, address the living, conjure the dead. Mother and sister, brother and son are at times interchangeable identities, avatars submitting to silence, death, the executioner of tulips. The tulips, like nearly all the primary images with which Celan has seeded his early poems, will be conserved through the harsh reductions of the last: In the wintry and exigent terrain of *Schneepart*, the tulip grows as a "Chalk-Crocus"—a calcified flower. In the penultimate poem of *Zeitgehöft*, the autumn perennial becomes a sign of timeless exile "seen / from the hospitable table." The lines near the end display a signpost revealing the title of Celan's volume *Von Schwelle zu Schwelle, From Threshold to Threshold*, a continuing practice of this poet, and evidence of the value he placed on a sequential and closely interrelated reading of his work.

The recognition accorded to *Von Schwelle zu Schwelle*, pub-

*The sting of self-accusation?

lished in 1955, and the immense celebrity of "Todesfuge" (a poem Celan apparently considered misused to the extent that he refused to allow its reprinting in a number of anthologies, save for an East German collection of Holocaust poems published in 1968) combined to award Celan the Bremen Prize for literature in 1958. His speech on this occasion, which provides the famous description of his poems as "messages in a bottle" which may or may not be retrieved, binds this utopian agenda for poetry to the memory of Osip Mandelstam. The metaphor of the "message in the bottle" appears in Mandelstam's essay "On the Interlocutor," which exclaims how providential is the force that drives the mariner's message in its glass bottle "across no matter how wide a sea into the hands of that one who is destined to find it." The composition of these "messages in a bottle," which Celan undertook from his own desert island, required that untiring application to language which the Bremen speech outlines: the poet going to language "with his very being, stricken by and seeking reality." Poem after poem from *Lichtzwang* will name this hard labor most succinctly: The charging of words with a transcendent reality takes place where

dusk has
the swimming word.

This resurrection of words—which Celan obliquely refers to in still another poem from *Lichtzwang* as

. . . him, the one
landing
word-beast

will see them pried apart, conjugated, babbled, stammered, trailed to catalepsis. Endlessly recombining words to yield the highest sum of their meanings, Celan commits himself to a "piling on of words, volcanic, drowned by the sea's roar."

The roar of the sea, the estranging distance between poet and reader, and the need for these poems to be read and reread over an extended period has given much of Celan's work after 1958 its reputation as a millenial object, a body of nearly impenetrable poems which might be accessible in a thousand years, as Hans-Georg Gadamer, who is representative of Celan's German critics, claims. But we can say, as T. S. Eliot said of Shakespeare, asserting that the full meaning of any one of his plays is not in the play alone, but in that play in the order in which it was written, in its relation to all of Shakespeare's other plays, that there is a lucid, precise, and intelligible pattern to these poems: They are shaped by an accountable lyric intelligence which drives their experience through a closely woven lattice formation. The thematic title of Celan's 1959 collection is *Sprachgitter*, a compound offering a wide spectrum of translations. Celan's translator Joachim Neugroschel chose *Speech-Grille*, an English conversion which focuses on its oldest and most concrete usage: the barred window or grating through which the cloistered spoke to outsiders. (In this context, it is essential to remember that the grate existed for the purpose of dialogue. Even in a prison cell, the grate is a device through which light, sound and air must pass.) The title also retains the philosophic concept of language as a grid which filters the expression of ideas. For fishermen, the *Gitter* is a trap or a net; in the physical sciences it denotes the lattice formation of the crystal. Barrier, net, grid, intricate action of time on stone or water, or metaphor for breath which freezes when expelled from the mouth, Celan's over-determined word comprises a class of objects whose structure is defined by their relationship to negative space. Its existence is shaped through the interpenetration of silence and emptiness.

In *Sprachgitter*, there is a stunning example of what is to come in Celan's work a decade later: We have a poem, dense with imagery and associations, which annihilates itself. "*Matière de Bretagne*," whose title weds the French word for suppurating matter, the product of physical decay, to the Arthurian cycle, deals with the erosion of myth, both sacred and secular, by the agency of time, in stanzas of great complexity recalling the Passion of Christ, the underwater bells of the drowned city of Ys, and the sail of the Tristan legend which announces (falsely) the death of the loved one, only in the final stanzas to be thus reduced:

> Gorselight, yellow, the slopes
> fester to heaven, the thorn
> courts the wound, bells are tolling
> down there, it is evening, the Void
> rolls its oceans to vespers
> the bloodsail is heading for you.
>
> . . . .
>
> Hands, the wound
> thorncourted, bells toll,
> hands, the Void, its oceans
> hands, in gorselight, the
> bloodsail
> is heading for you.

```
You
     you teach
     you teach your hands
     you teach your hands you teach
     you teach your hands
                         to sleep.
   (TR. WASHBURN-GUILLEMIN)
```

We are watching the vanishing trick, the folding of the page, within the poem itself. The poem is made and by the maker's slight of hand, unmade. This is a process which Mallarmé, in his last published poem, *"Un Coup de dés,"* "A Dice Throw," invoked through the establishment of "white spaces." Mallarmé expressed the hope, in the preface to the "Dice Throw," that the genre—his attenuated *vers libre*, foreshortened, motile, accelerated, and stripped of the conventions of versification would

> laisse intact l'antique vers, auquel je garde un culte et attribue l'empire de la passion et des rêveries.

> ("leave intact the older verse forms, which I worship and consider the realm of passion and dreams")

The Celan of 1959, of *"Matière de Bretagne,"* ransacking a concordance of Rilkean compounds, is still Mallarmé's poet, calling for the repose of writing hands, a release from prayer: "You teach your hands to sleep." Sleep is still the irrational realm in which truth can be perceived anew. Sleeping, dreaming—the dream, like a lattice, filters waking experience, creates a mesh of word-play, association, and memory through which we drift and fall and rise once more. Ten years later, in *Lichtzwang*, which may have been composed around the time of one of Celan's stays in a French mental hospital, we find the excruciating line: "To go into the straddle of sleep o once."

There is a temporary respite from these struggles in Celan's next book. *Niemandsrose* is a cycle of poems dedicated to Osip Mandelstam. Whether it was the short truce with the German language, the identification with that most affirmative of doomed poets, Mandelstam, or the energy and order drawn from the cosmic Gnostic drama of Kabbalism which these poems articulate with growing force, Celan made a half-turn back toward the lyric expansiveness, the melodic fluency and ease of his earlier work. Although he states in *Sibirisch*, a poem which never directly mentions Mandelstam:

> I too
> have the thousand-year colored
> stone in my throat,

we are compelled to reconcile this bitter jibe at the language of the Thousand-Year Reich with the recollection that, in classical antiquity, speaking with a mouth filled with stones, an image in Celan for the poetic utterance, was the remedy of choice for stammering. Following the example of Mandelstam, digging in the earth for the pure word under its damaged counterfeits, and of Mallarmé, whose poet is a seraph with a flaming sword giving *"un sens plus pur aux mots de la tribe"* ("a greater purity of meaning to the words of the group"), Celan found a temporary equipoise between speech and silence, an integration and consolidation of his poetic gifts.

But the hard-won resolution of *Niemandsrose* proved too

fragile to contain forever Celan's unstable pact with the German language. With *Atemwende*, or *Breath-Turning*, published in 1967, and *Fadensonnen*, *Thread-Suns*, published in 1968, the struggle for expression, coupled with the yearning for transcendence, which these two titles propose, moved into an acute phase. As Michael Hamburger has observed, breath units, rather than metrical or syllabic ones, begin to govern the movement of the poem. Acoustic values are altered. At times we have something closely mimicking an asthmatic rattle as the musical accompaniment to the slow demolition of Celan's lattice structure, the paring down to its essential elements. The heavily iambic rhythms fade from the text; the genitival metaphors which bear the inflections of Eluard and Goll are replaced by paradox, and by negative tropes which deliver arguments *in extremis*. As Celan remarks in a late poem in *Lichtzwang*, which seems to renounce the work of certain contemporaries and the repetition of forms which they exemplify:

> If I gobbled up the wagon-ruts,
> I'd be on my way.

The rich deposits of Rilkean compounds are crossed by more abrasive syllables, while the Apollonian music of other predecessors is increasingly paid the ironic homage of mockery. The tempi are speeded up, the notation itself changes. The use of punctuation to elucidate a complex syntax dwindles: The poetic line is bent out of its usual contour by such an assault on syntax that even German readers are baffled by its departure from plain linear progression and mark its wrenching into more sharply concentrated forms. There is a willed disorder in placement values, in the location of individual parts. Units of meaning are smaller and less uniform in shape. Lines are shorter, or they grind to an echolalic halt. Here and there are great rents in the grid itself. Above all, there is a rise in the frequency of very short poems.

Until *Atemwende*, Celan was the skilled practitioner of the art of the *Widerruf*, the refutation of a given poem (often Rilke's) by one of his own. The late poems begin to dismantle even that scaffolding, exposing the poet's deep resolve to unify his linguistic cosmogony. By forcing the flood of colors, images, and tonalities of his earlier work through a series of narrowing locks, Celan creates a parallel universe of language, raging with silence, clamorous with meaning. He takes German poetry through a process which Clarence Brown identifies with Mandelstam: a willed decomposition, in which a stylistic devolution "creates out of its own wreck the thing it contemplates."

Celan's poems, exclusive of *Zeitgehöft*, the last of his posthumous volumes translated in this book, exist in a standard two-volume edition in German. The first volume, containing all of his poems through *Niemandsrose*, displays a fragment from an early poem on the back cover: ". . . At the eastern window, the slender wanderer-phantom of feeling appears at night." The second volume begins with *Atemwende*, a turning of the breath, which not only points us due north, toward the "wintering over" which its contents delineate, but also suggest the notion, well-known to Celan, who was an acquaintance of Gershom Scholem, of the Lurianic Kabbalists, of the

*Zimzum.** The word describes the act of divine contraction
that preceded emanations, the moment of God's breathing in
so as to make room for his creation—its consequence being
the absence of God in the fallen world, a negative theology
elaborated by the similar reticence of the maker of the poems
in this volume and its successors.

> Sometimes, however,
> the sky dies
> ahead of
> our shards.

In the second volume we are pulled within the visionary
borders of Celan's late poems, where familiar things have
fallen away. As if to underscore the difficulty and strangeness
of this place where Celan's most gifted translators began to
lay down their pens, the use of discrete titles for the poems,
set above and apart from the text, is diminishing. He chooses,
instead, to identify a poem by the orthographic practice of
setting an opening phrase in upper case, a singular configu-
ration which is something more than private signature or
anti-rhetorical flourish. The omission of conventional titles
is perhaps intended as a severe nonreferential gesture, con-
forming to the inscription on the cover of the second volume
of the Suhrkamp edition: *"Die Welt ist fort. Ich muss dich tra-*

*"How did He produce and create this world? Like a man who gathers
in and contracts his breath, so that the smaller might contain the larger,
so He contracted His light into a hand's breadth, according to His Own
measure, and the world was left in darkness, and in that darkness He cut
boulders and hewed rocks."

gen." ("The world is gone. I must carry you"). With these words we enter a poetic enclosure of great transparency and light, where things, like the poem, name themselves.

II

Though the brevity of these pieces is a persuasive advocate for them, on the other hand that very brevity itself requires an advocate.   SCHÖNBERG ON WEBERN

We have mentioned silence in Webern; let us add that this feature is one of the most irritant and provocative in his work. One of the truths hardest to demonstrate is that music is not just the 'Art of sound'—that it must be defined rather as a counterpoint of sound and silence. Webern's one, unique, rhythmic innovation is this conception whereby sound and silence are linked in a precise organization directed toward the exhaustive exploitation of our powers of hearing. The tension of sound is enriched to the extent of a genuine respiration, comparable only with Mallarmé's contribution to poetry.   PIERRE BOULEZ, *The Threshold*

Solitude, récif, étoile
A n'importe ce qui valut
La blanc sourci de notre toile.
                    MALLARMÉ

("Solitude, star, rock-coast
to that no matter which
worth the white concern of our sail."
                    TR. C. F. MACINTYRE.)

We know little of the personal crises, deepened and prolonged as they were by the damage of Celan's past, which rekindled the distrust of language that flares up again with such brilliance in these final poems. There is a story that Edmond Jabès once found Celan frantically stuffing his mailbox with a borrowed manuscript of *The Book of Questions*. The poet, who had previously expressed some interest in translating it, informed Jabès that the publication of such a book, with its direct treatment of Jewish themes, would bring fresh catastrophe on all of them. The poet's fear that directness rendered his utterance ephemeral may have found its psychic counterpart in the troubled survivor's fear of renewed persecution and reprisal. The diction of these poems, while reducing the past into images of shadow, smoke, and snow, simultaneously begins to lock in the words "delusion," "madness," and "pain." Near the bottom of a two page *vita* recording the central dates of Celan's life and work in the collection of studies "Über Paul Celan", we find the terse notation: "April, 1970. *Freitod in der Seine*," followed by a list of three posthumous volumes of poems. *Freitod*, the German literary word for suicide, which blends the language's capacity for euphemism and invention, is suggestive of the kind of verbal coinage which engaged Celan so profoundly in these last poems, and which he employed in their virtually untranslatable titles.

The process of publishing the first volume, *Lichtzwang*, which can be rendered by nothing more proximate then *Light-Force*, a solution which sacrifices half a dozen resonances, was underway at the time of the poet's death. It appeared in print later that same year, each of its eighty-eight poems set in the precise sequence to which Celan attached such importance. The text of the second, *Schneepart*, was located in a meticulously edited fair copy, and saw publication in 1971. *Schneepart* can be more adequately translated as "Snow-Part," a word which refers, in a technical sense, to the part written for the voice of snow in a musical composition— witness to the polyphony of Celan's silence.* A final volume, *Zeitgehöft*, did not appear until 1976, its contents assembled from three sheaves of poems associated with Celan's trip to Israel in 1969. When we crack apart the German compound, we then extract, for the transfer with English, *Zeit*, or Time, and *Gehöft*, a word from Austrian dialect which yields *Farm-stead*. *The Farmstead of Time* will meet our English purpose, but the American "homestead" may bring us closer to the deepest sounding of the German word.

The ninety-nine poems translated here were selected from these final three volumes: *Light-Force*, *Snow-Part*, and *The Farmstead of Time*. The great majority of these are small poems, speaking little, saying everything. The special rigors of their radical language-economy raise, however obliquely, the same dangerous question which the music of Webern posed, and poses still, to the most admiring of audiences. What music can be written after this? What other forward motion is possible for the art itself? Adorno claimed, in a remark too often cited, that after the barbarism of Ausch-witz, there could be no more poems. Celan's work has re-futed that claim while stealthily supplanting it with another, to which there is still no adequate reply: After Celan's poems, after their risky journey into what a German critic has called

*The English language, unfortunately, cannot house every implication of the German title. *Parte*, James Lyon reminds us, is in Austrian dialect the word for *Todesanzeige*—obituary.

"the nomansland between speech and silence," what new explorations can be made?—"Where do you go / when the going's nowhere?" The posthumous issue of this poet, in which poetic speech is taken to its limit, may truly deserve the collective title its present translators have given it. These are, in every sense, last poems.

Nonetheless, they may not require the special advocacy for their brevity which Schönberg thought necessary for the *Opus Six* of Webern. Fifty intervening years of culture have reconciled us to the minimal and acquainted us with its virtues. Just as in desert places the sculptural qualities of plants emerge, so does the brittle, hardened and uncompromising landscape of Celan's late poems yield the last harvest of his poetic vocabulary, in which the word is as clearly etched and distinct as a fossil leaf. It is through whatever sustained attention we are capable of bringing to these words, this crop of leaves turned to stone, that we learn to read these poems.

The translator, shabby double agent in the linguistic field, shuttling between two borders, anxiously consulting with his native guide and weighing one betrayal against another, derives some final profit from his calculations: The advantage of that long scrutiny which the poet recommended to his biographer. Filaments of meaning which brachiate from poem to poem are outlined with an intense clarity so that the "poppy-capsule," the sedative substance which injures language in "DREAM-DRIVEN," is paradoxically linked to the dream-flower of the earlier poems. Clusters of associations assemble around a word translated nine times, taken thereby to the nth power. Celan's wordgames, his visual puns and *trompe l'oeil*, the elaborate play of homophones from text to text, have, for the translator, their most vivid impact through his own failure: we focus on the casualties of the process, the quarry of the hunt which eluded our tireless plots and simulations and finally bounded right off the map so meticulously shaded black for German, white for English. It is no accident that contemporary translators' argot employs the term "target language."

The virtuosity, the immense resources of the English language, can absorb only partially the depth of the investment Celan has made in his nouns, or the facility he has given to his adverbs of time and space. Translating the first line of the first poem in this collection, one is stunned by the resonance of *Muschelhaufen*: a word bearing the burden of multiple meanings and associations essential to Celan's work. The heap of mussel-shells must become sea-shells, if any metrical conformity is to be attained. The linguistic information available to a German speaker with a modest aquaintance with natural science—the fact that the crushed fossil remains of mussels result in limestone formations which are a central feature of the topography of many of these late poems must be scanted: Leaps of interpretation, however seductive and well-realized, may reveal the translator's *hubris*. Similarly, this translation cannot provide another essential allusion in this or many another poem: Celan's shells are often their Hebrew equivalent, the *kelippot*, which are shells, husks, or shards of evil, which, in Kabbalistic mythology, dominate those captured lights from a flawed Genesis awaiting restoration. Those captured lights, according to Gershom Scholem, provide the life-force for the entire world of corrupt things. They lend a contraction of their name, *Licht-*

zwang, *Light-Force*, to the volume which houses this poem. There is no possible evasion of the sense of menace, despair, and anguished paradox that invades much of the work of *Lichtzwang* and *Schneepart*. In a poem written under the axe, which literally begins:

HATCHET-SWARMS
above us

conversations
with long-muzzled axes in lowland

we suppose that Celan is recalling one of his many troubled and anxiety-ridden encounters with those Germans whom he both esteemed and feared. Surely love and loathing conspired in his relationship with Heidegger, who might well, in a moment of rage, be named as a long-muzzled axe in *Tiefland*, the name given to an allegorized Germany in a forgotten novel. But even this indictment is softened: Celan, the stranded mariner, becomes his own desert island, one which is, paradoxically, a fertile place:

you, island-meadow,
you yourself
fogged in with
hope.

Just as Rilke is the poet with whom Celan, insofar as he can abandon the lacerating quarrel which he wages against himself, is engaged in the most ambivalent of dialogues, Heidegger is the philosopher who is doubly the object of spleen and veneration. In the enigmatic six line poem which begins "LEFT BACK FOR ME," Heidegger is the adversary whose provocation jolts the poet into an increasingly rare assertion of the first person. An "I" emerges, to unravel the riddle, while "you," an ambiguous figure, clothed in hempcloth, a fabric suggestive of the hangman's rope, knits "the stocking of mystery." Günter Grass's novel *Dog Years*, which devotes a long section to a scathing parody-pastiche of Heidegger's metaphysical jargon, supplied the allusion: Heidegger, the supporter of National Socialism, who affected the stocking cap of the simple Alemannic peasant, is summed up in Grass's sneering reference to the "stocking cap of phenomenology." In this short poem, meanings inescapably converge. The phenomenologist's philosophical activity is meshed with the plaiting of the hangman's noose.

This shuttle between dark and light in *Lichtzwang* allows more access to the translator than the brilliant derangements of sound and sense which dominate the glacial territory of *Schneepart*. This selection, accordingly, comprises twice as many poems from the former: in *Lichtzwang*, the translator, more sure of himself as reader, can count on the German text on the left-hand side of the page to compensate for the more conventional failures of his craft. The reader of this book will miss, in the translation offered here of:

ANGEREMPELT beim Wahngang
von einem, der las:
Grind und Schorf. Schorf und Grind.

In die Schlafgrätsche gehn, o einmal.

a replication in English of Celan's consonantal zeugma in the last line: The initial phonemes of *Grind* and *Schorf* are yoked together in *Schlafgrätsche*, a recombination of verbal elements which obliquely reminds us of the troubled character of that longed-for sleep, in which the wound, though crusted over, persists.

Hence, the bilingual edition is utterly indispensible in the case of this poet. It is hoped that the reader who gives the utmost attention to those verbal effects which are sacrificed by their English doubles will be as indulgent toward the successes achieved at the expense of strict fidelity as he is toward the casualties inflicted on the same account. The relative intactness and fluidity of the poetic line typical of *Lichtzwang* afforded the occasional possibility of making these difficult choices, where the taut, choppy line of *Schneepart*, its lacerated syntax, lacunae, hesitations, aphaisic fumblings and epileptic halts, made decisions of this kind an unattainable luxury. In a climate of scarcity, there are fewer transactions between natives and outlanders. Puzzling over a particularly intractable poem from *Schneepart*, one thinks of those texts of the archaic Greek poets, of a fragment of Alcman, so badly mutilated in transmission that what survived was, in fact, a column of half lines. The torn page was readable only when restored by the scholar's fine manipulations.

With *Zeitgehöft*, however, we seem to find ourselves once more in a world of partial grace, under a less inhuman light. We can speculate that perhaps Celan's stay in Israel in 1960 accomplished some of that same release and renewed ease with his natural lyricism that the retrieval of his Jewish heritage lent to the earlier *Niemandsrose*. The prediction ventured in "NO HAND HOLDS ME, I was born like you," from *Lichtzwang*, of the blossoming of Jewish seed—literally the almond-testicle—is fulfilled in Celan's vision of Israel. Playing on the German words for east and west, *Morgenland* and *Abendland*, he locates the Middle Eastern homeland of the Jews in the "afternoon." In "FROM THE SINKING WHALE-BROW," an opening line possibly alluding to the floundering Leviathan of the West, a six-pointed star is salvaged—a scrap of comfort—from the sea's wreck.

Schneepart is not a book ample in such solace. In *Lichtzwang* the poem is still a "lark-shaped stone," or a "leaf-green"—that is, time-colored, "shadow." (But the poem is then only the shadow of an image: something closer to extinction.) Although the island in *Lichtzwang*, the acre of sea-soned silence, appears like Van Gogh's last self-portrait, "in the flame," the heated anguish of *Lichtzwang* is somehow less estranging than the snow-conversations of *Schneepart*. The pure and transcendent words of *Schneepart* finally reveal themselves as elements in a conversation with the dead. Nonetheless, they are conversations that command our attention and ask to be overheard:

> FROM THE BEAM
> come in like the night
> the last sail
> billows,
>
> on board
> your scream
> enshrined
> you were there, you are below,
> you are down below,
>
> . . . .
>
> with the drop-keel
> I get a reading from you.

The word in its last extremity, like the *Notsegel* or emergency sail, still moves this vessel, the shrine of screams which are reachable only by writing fingers. The double-entendre of the last two lines manages not only the nautical statement but a positive assertion of the poet. No conversion of *Schwertkiel* into English can convey its symbolic force. The generic qualifier for keel, *Schwert*, is a sword, and the keel, *Kiel* in German, is also a quill-pen, and an instrument of writing, which will re-emerge in *Zeitgehöft*, where, having evoked the filaments and stars central to his creation with "hatching of grubs, hatching of stars," Celan closes by saying:

> with every
> keel
> I search for you
> fathomless.

The labors of the contemporary scholiasts who are presently assembling a critical edition of Paul Celan's work are still incomplete. We are left, then, to read these poems in the uneasy knowledge that our recognition of the mass of allusions, ideas, fractured quotations, and references on which a full understanding would depend, is only partial and imperfect. The range of associations, even in *Last Poems* (opacity was not a principle of selection) includes Whitman, the Gospels, the Tenth Duino Elegy, the Kabbalistic theory of left-side Emenations, Christopher Marlowe, Jacobin argot, the events of 1968 in Paris and a good recall of Celan's *Meridian* address. But to read these poems it is not necessary to cross-reference the universe of the written word. We have only to focus, with a meditative will, on Celan's words, on their intersections with each other and on the constellations they form in the stillness around them. The individual word survives to repay our scrutiny and to justify the violence of the measures undertaken to preserve it. Celan employed the most rigorous of means to protect his history and his experience from trivialization, no doubt anticipating a future in which "Auschwitz," and "genocide" would lose their potency and turn into threadbare metaphor. The coiner of words looked not only at the debasement of the currency which preceded him, but foresaw that which lay ahead. He has given us instead a host of invulnerable signs. Nothing violates the white concern of this sail.

Another artificer of language, fifty years before, chose the triple strategy of "silence, exile, and cunning." Celan's was the silence of the unutterable, his exile a flight from the unforgiveable, his cunning the craft of high art.

KATHARINE WASHBURN

INHALTSVERZEICHNIS

aus *Lichtzwang* (1970)

CONTENTS

from *Force of Light* (1970)

aus *Schneepart* (1971)

from *Snow-Part* (1971)

aus *Zeitgehöft* (1976)

from *Farmstead of Time* (1976)

LAST POEMS

Lichtzwang

Force of Light

MUSCHELHAUFEN: mit
der Geröllkeule fuhr ich dazwischen,
den Flüssen folgend in die ab-
schmelzende Eis-
heimat,
zu ihm, dem nach wessen
Zeichen zu ritzenden
Feuerstein im
Zwergbirkenhauch.

Lemminge wühlten.

Kein Später.

Keine
Schalenurne, keine
Durchbruchscheibe,
keine Sternfuß-
Fibel.

Ungestillt,
unverknüpft, kunstlos,
stieg das Allverwandelnde langsam
schabend
hinter mir her.

Heap of sea-shells: I
intervened with the gravel-club,
following the floods to the final
iceland
melting
towards it, towards the
firestone that must be engraved
with someone's sign
in the trace of dwarf-birches.

Lemmings burrowed.

No Later.

No
shell-urn, no
pane for breaching,
no brooch
of star-feet.

Unappeased,
unattached, artless,
what alters the universe came up slowly
rasping
behind me.

MIT DER ASCHENKELLE GESCHÖPFT
aus dem Seinstrog,
seifig, im
zweiten
Ansatz, auf-
einanderhin,

unbegreiflich geatzt jetzt,
weit
außerhalb unser und schon——weshalb?——
auseinandergehoben,

dann (im dritten
Ansatz?) hinters
Horn geblasen, vor das
stehende
Tränentrumm,
einmal, zweimal, dreimal,

aus unpaariger,
knospend-gespaltener,
fahniger
Lunge.

SERVED WITH THE ASH-LADLE
from the trough of being,
silty, at the
second
start, towards
each other,

now corroded beyond comprehension,
far
beyond us and already—wherefore?—
heaved asunder,

then (at the third
start?) blown
behind the horn, before the
enduring
clot of tears,
once, twice, thrice,

from an unpaired,
burgeoning-cleft,
flag-like
lung.

IN DIE NACHT GEGANGEN, helferisch,
ein stern-
durchlässiges Blatt
statt des Mundes:

es bleibt
noch etwas wild zu vertun,
bäumlings.

GONE INTO THE NIGHT, complicit,
a star-
porous leaf
for a mouth:

something remains
for wild wasting,
treeward.

TRETMINEN auf deinen linken
Monden, Saturn.

Scherbenversiegelt
die Umlaufbahnen dort draußen.

Es muß jetzt der Augenblick sein
für eine gerechte
Geburt.

CONTACT-MINES on your left
moons, Saturn.

Sealed against shards
the orbits out there.

Now is the hour
for a righteous
birth.

WER SCHLUG SICH ZU DIR?
Der lerchengestaltige
Stein aus der Brache.
Kein Ton, nur das Sterbelicht trägt
an ihm mit.

Die Höhe
wirbelt sich
aus, heftiger noch
als ihr.

WHO GOT TO YOUR SIDE?
The lark-shaped
stone from the fallow land.
No sound, only the light for the deathwatch helps
bear it along.

The heights
whirl themselves away
still more fiercely
than you.

ABGLANZBELADEN, bei den
Himmelskäfern,
im Berg.

Den Tod,
den du mir schuldig bliebst, ich
trag ihn
aus.

LADEN WITH REFLECTION, with
the sky-beetles,
inside the mountain.

The death
you still owe me, I
carry it
out.

FREIGEGEBEN auch dieser
Start.

Bugradgesang mit
Corona.

Das Dämmerruder spricht an,
deine wach-
gerissene Vene
knotet sich aus,

was du noch bist, legt sich schräg,
du gewinnst
Höhe.

CLEARED for this
departure too.

Song of the front wheel with
corona.

The rudder of dusk engages you,
your slit-
awake vein
untangles,

what's left of you, sets itself aslant,
you gain
altitude.

BAKEN-
sammler, nächtlings,
die Hucke voll,
am Fingerende den Leitstrahl,
für ihn, den einen an-
fliegenden
Wortstier.

Baken-
meister.

COLLECTOR
of beacons, at night,
your pack full,
at your fingertip the guiding beam,
for him, the one
landing
word-beast.

Master
of beacons.

AUS VERLORNEM Gegossene du,
maskengerecht,

die Lid-
falte entlang
mit der eignen
Lidfalte dir nah sein,

die Spur und die Spur
mit Grauem bestreun,
endlich, tödlich.

FROM THINGS LOST you were cast,
perfect the mask,

along the fold
of your eyelid
in the fold of my own
close to you,

the spoor, the spoor
strew it with gray,
final, deathly.

EINMAL, der Tod hatte Zulauf,
verbargst du dich in mir.

ONCE, when death was mobbed,
you took shelter in me.

BEILSCHWÄRME
über uns,

Gespräche
mit Tüllenäxten im Tiefland—

Inselflur du,
mit der dich
übernebelnden
Hoffnung.

HATCHET-SWARMS
above us,

conversations
with long-muzzled axes in lowland—

you, island-meadow,
you yourself
fogged-in with
hope.

VORGEWUSST blutet
zweimal hinter dem Vorhang,

Mitgewußt
perlt

FOREKNOWLEDGE bleeds
twice behind the curtain,

knowledge shared
sheds pearls

Wo ICH mich in dir vergaß,
wardst du Gedanke,

etwas
rauscht durch uns beide:
der Welt erste
der letzten
Schwingen,

mir wächst
das Fell zu überm
gewittrigen
Mund,

du
kommst nicht
zu
dir.

WHERE I forgot myself in you,
you became idea,

something
rushes through us both:
the world's first
of the last
wings,

my hide
spreads over my
storm-weathered
mouth,

you
come not
to
you.

SEIT LANGEM bestiegener Schlammkahn.

Ein ab-
gesprungener
Knopf
tüftelt an jeder Ranunkel,

die Stunde, die Kröte,
hebt ihre Welt aus den Angeln.

Wenn ich die Karrenspur fräße,
wär ich dabei.

MIRE-BOAT long since boarded.

A stud
snapped-off
quibbles
with every buttercup,

the hour, the toad,
turns its world upside down.

If I gobbled up the wagon-ruts,
I'd be on my way.

SINK mir weg
aus der Armbeuge,

nimm den Einen
Pulsschlag mit,

verbirg dich darin,
draußen.

SINK out of
the crook of my arm,

take the One
pulse beat along,

hide yourself within,
out there.

ANGEREMPELT beim Wahngang
von einem, der las:
Grind und Schorf. Schorf und Grind.

In die Schlafgrätsche gehn, o einmal.

GOADED on the mad-road
by someone who read:
Scab and scurf. Scurf and scab.

To go into the straddle of sleep, o once.

BLITZGESCHRECKT, unverwandelt, kaum
gesträubt:
                Géricaults
                        Pferd,
                                schon
von deinen Nadelblicken geheilt
über und über.

Noch hier in diesem
Gewitter
reitest du's zu.

Ein Trittstein, noch fern deinem Fuß,
winkt mit der einen
rötlichen
Strähne aus meinem Bart.

LIGHTNING-SHOCKED, unchanged, scarcely
ruffled:
        Géricault's
              horse,
                     already
healed by your needle-glances
over and over.

Even here in this
thunderstorm
you break it in.

A stepping-stone, still far from your foot,
waves with the one
reddish
strand from my beard.

WURFSCHEIBE, mit
Vorgesichten besternt,

wirf dich

aus dir hinaus.

DISCUS,
starred with premonitions,

throw yourself

out of yourself.

KLOPF die
Lichtkeile weg:

das schwimmende Wort
hat der Dämmer.

CHISEL OFF the
bolts of light:

dusk has
the swimming word.

DIE ENTSPRUNGENEN
Graupapageien
lesen die Messe
in deinem Mund.

Du hörsts regnen
und meinst, auch diesmal
sei's Gott.

HAVING ESCAPED
the gray parrots
recite Mass
in your mouth.

You hear the rain
and think, this time, too,
it's God.

IN DEN DUNKELSCHLÄGEN erfuhr ichs:

du lebst auf mich zu, dennoch,
im Steigrohr,
im
Steigrohr.

DURING THE DARK BLOWS I found out:

you live towards me, nonetheless,
in the standpipe,
in the
standpipe.

STREUBESITZ, staub-
unmittelbar.

Abend um Abend schweben
die den Gedanken entzognen
Botschaften ein,
königshart, nachthart,
in die Hände der Klage-
vögte:

aus dem Knick
ihrer Lebens-
linien
tritt lautlos die Antwort:
der eine ewige
Tropfen
Gold.

DESMEGNE OF LITTER, urgent
as dust.

Evening after evening, embassies
drift over, distilled
from thoughts,
hard as kings, hard as night,
into the hands of the grief-
constables:

from the break
in their life-
lines
the answer steps soundless:
the one eternal
drop of
gold.

DER VON DEN UNBESCHRIEBENEN
Blättern
abgelesene Brief,

der Totstell-Reflexe
grausilberne Kette darauf,
gefolgt von drei silbernern
Takten.

Du weißt: der Sprung
geht über dich, immer.

FROM THE UNWRITTEN
pages
the letter read,

the silver-gray chain on it,
reflexes of sham-death,
followed by three silvered
beats.

You know: the leap
goes over you, forever.

SCHNEID DIE GEBETSHAND
aus
der Luft
mit der Augen-
schere,
kapp ihre Finger
mit deinem Kuß:

Gefaltetes geht jetzt
atemberaubend vor sich.

CUT THE PRAYER-HAND
from
the air
with the eye-
shears,
lop its fingers off
with your kiss:

Now a folding takes place
that takes your breath away.

WAS ES AN STERNEN BEDARF,
schüttet sich aus,

deiner Hände laubgrüner Schatten
sammelt es ein,

freudig zerbeiß ich
das münzenkernige
Schicksal.

WHAT IS NEEDED WHEN SPEAKING OF STARS
sheds itself,

the leaf-green shadow of your hands
gathers it,

gladly I bite off
nugget after nugget of
fate.

IM LEEREN
wo sich die Kuttel rankt
mit der Bregen-
Blüte,
warf ich mich Steinen zu,
die fingen mich auf
und bekrönten ein Rund
mit dem, was ich wurde.

IN EMPTY SPACE
where entrails entwine
with the cerebral
blossom,
I cast myself to stones,
they caught me
and ringed a sphere
with what I became.

DIE LEHMIGEN OPFERGÜSSE,
von Schnecken umkrochen:

das Bild der Welt,
dem Himmel entgegengetragen
auf einem Brombeerblatt.

THE LOAMY GUSH OF SACRIFICE
encircled by snails:

the image of the world,
carried heavenwards
on a bramble leaf.

Das Wildherz, verhäuslicht
vom halbblinden Stich

in die Lunge,

Veratmetes sprudelt,

langsam, blutunterwaschen
konfiguriert sich
das selten verheißne
rechte
Neben-
leben.

THE WILD-HEART, domesticated
by a half-blind stab

into the lung,

Air gushes forth,

slowly, soaked with blood
shapes itself
into the rare promise of
authentic
side-
life.

HERZSCHALL-FIBELN, eingezäunt,

das Kranichpaar
denkt sich dir vor,

aspektral
verschenkt sich das Licht deiner Blume,

dem Fangbein der Mantis
begegnet dein über-
sterniges
Immer.

PRIMERS OF PULSE-SOUND, hedged in,

the pair of cranes
you imagine,

aspectral
the light of your flower gives itself away,

the clawfoot of the mantis
meets your starred-
over
Forever.

ANEINANDER
müde geworden,
randgängerisch,
mündig,

Luft
schaufelt sich zu, auch
Wasser,

die Kartenschlägerin klebt
erschlagen hinterm
Herz-As.

GROWN WEARY
of each other,
roaming the edge,
come of age,

air
adjoins itself, and
water too,

the card-reader slain
cleaves to
the ace of hearts.

DIE MIR HINTERLASSNE
balkengekreuzte
Eins:

an ihr soll ich rätseln,
während du, im Rupfengewand,
am Geheimnisstrumpf strickst.

LEFT BACK FOR ME
cross-beamed
One:

the riddle I must unravel,
while you, in hempcloth,
knit the stocking of mystery.

MAGNETISCHE BLÄUE im Mund,
erkeuchst du Pol um Pol,

gesömmerter Schnee
wirft sich drüber,

bald hängt der taumlige Star
im doppelten Liedschwarm.

BLUE OF THE LODES in your mouth,
you gasp up pole after pole,

snow summered over
throws itself on it,

soon the drunken starling reels
in the double swarm of songs.

VORFLUT
kämmt deine Algen zusammen,
legt sie
um dich.
Eingedämmt wuchert,
was du noch hast.

Ein weißer Stirnsplitter geht
für dich über die Grenze.

PRE-FLOOD
combs your algae together,
lays them
around you.
What you still have
spreads dammed in.

A white brow-splinter goes
for you over the border.

DIE MANTIS, wieder,
im Nacken des Worts,
in das du geschlüpft warst—,

muteinwärts
wandert der Sinn,
sinneinwärts
der Mut.

THE MANTIS, once more
at the neck of the word,
into which you slipped—,

courageward
wanders the mind,
mindward
courage.

ANREDSAM
war die ein-
flüglig schwebende Amsel,
über der Brandmauer, hinter
Paris, droben,
im
Gedicht.

APPROACHABLE
the one-
winged soaring blackbird,
above the firewall, behind
Paris, up there,
in the
poem.

Mir wuchs Zinn in die Hand,
ich wußte mir nicht
zu helfen:
modeln mochte ich nicht,
lesen mocht es mich nicht—

Wenn sich jetzt
Ossietzkys letzte
Trinkschale fände,
ließ ich das Zinn
von ihr lernen,

und das Heer der Pilger-
stäbe
durchschwiege, durchstünde die Stunde.

Oranienstrasse 1

Tin sprouted in my hand,
I did not know what
to do:
I had no wish to mould,
it had no wish to read me—

If now
Ossietzky's last
drinking vessel could be found,
I would let the tin
learn from it,

and the host of pilgrims'
staffs
would distill silence, still survive the hour.

MIT TRAUMANTRIEB auf der Kreisbahn,
an-
geschwelt,

zwei Masken statt einer,
Planetenstaub in den gehöhlten
Augen,

nachtblind, tagblind,
weltblind,

die Mohnkapsel in dir
geht irgendwo nieder,
beschweigt
einen Mitstern,

die schwimmende Trauerdomäne
vermerkt einen weiteren Schatten,

es helfen dir alle,

der Herzstein durchstößt seinen Fächer,
keinerlei
Kühle,

es helfen dir alle,

du segelst, verglimmst und verglost,

DREAM-DRIVEN on the cir-
cular track,
swollen,

two masks for one,
the dust of planets in hollowed
eyes,

nightblind, dayblind,
worldblind,

the poppy-capsule within you
goes down somewhere,
silences
a fellow star,

the swimming domain of sorrow
records another shadow,

it all does you good,

the heartstone thrusts through its fan,
no cooling
at all,

it all does you good,

you sail, smoulder, and die down,

Augenschwärme passieren die Enge,
ein Blutkloß schwenkt ein auf die Bahn,
Erdschwärme sprechen dir zu,

das Wetter im All
hält Ernte.

swarms of eyes pass the straits,
a blood clot enters the track,
swarms of earth encourage you,

all the weather in the universe
is harvesting.

FÜR DEN LERCHENSCHATTEN
brachgelegt das Verborgne,

un-
verhärtet
eingebracht die erfahrene
Stille, ein Acker, inslig,
im Feuer,

nach der
abgesättigten Hoffnung,
nach allem
abgezweigten Geschick:

die unbußfertig ersungenen
Moosopfer, wo du

mich suchst, blindlings.

FOR THE SHADOW OF THE LARK
the secret is untilled,

un-
hardened
harvested the seasoned
silence, an acre, like an island
in the flame,

after the
hope fed to fullness,
after all
the fork-pathed fate:

the moss-offering, sung
without contrition, where you

are seeking me, blindfold.

DER DURCHSCHNITTENE Taubenkordon,
die gesprengten
Blütengewalten,

die tatverdächtige
Fundsache Seele.

THE CORDON OF DOVES cut through,
the blasted
powers of blossoms,

charged with misdeed
the sought-for thing, soul.

SCHALLTOTES SCHWESTERGEHÄUS,
laß die Zwerglaute ein,
die ausgefragten:
sie mummeln das Großherz zusammen
und tragen es huckepack zu
jeder Not, jeder Not.

Sound-dead sister-shell,
let the dwarf-sounds in,
they have been examined:
together they muffle up the great heart
and bear it off on their shoulders to
every distress, every distress.

Im Zeitwinkel schwört
die entschleierte Erle
still vor sich hin,

auf dem Erdrücken, handspannenbreit,
hockt die durchschossene
Lunge,

an der Flurgrenze pickt
die Flügelstunde das Schneekorn
aus dem eigenen Steinaug,

Lichtbänder stecken mich an,
Kronschäden flackern.

IN THE CORNER OF TIME
the alder revealed
swears to itself in stillness,

on the back of the earth, breadth of a handspan,
squats the lung
shot through,

at the edge of fields the winged hour
plucks the grain of snow
from its own eye of stone.

Streamers of light infect me,
Flaws in the crown flicker.

AUCH MICH, den wie du Geborenen, hält keine Hand,
und keine wirft mir ein Glück in die Stunde, nicht anders als dir,
dem wie ich in Stierblut Getauchten,

doch stehen die Zahlen bereit, der Träne zu leuchten,
die in die Welt schnellt
aus unserm Nabel,

doch geht in die große Silbenschrift ein,
was uns nah kam, einzeln,

und die Mandelhode
gewittert
und blüht.

No HAND holds me, I was born like you,
and not one throws luck into my hour, it's no different for you,
you, washed as I was, in the blood of the steer,

but the numbers stand ready to light the tear,
bursting into the world
from our navel,

but what came near us, alone,
becomes part of the great script of syllables,

and the sack of almond seed
thunders
and blooms.

DIE RÜCKWÄRTSGESPROCHENEN
Namen, alle,

der äußerste, zum
König gewiehert
vor Rauhreifspiegeln,

umlagert, umstellt
von Mehrlingsgeburten,

der Zinnenriß durch ihn,
der dich Vereinzelten
mitmeint.

ALL THE NAMES
spoken backward,

the ultimate one
whinnied into a king
before frost-rimed mirrors,

beleaguered, besieged
by multiple births,

through it the breach of battlement,
which includes you
isolate.

SPERRTONNENSPRACHE, Sperrtonnenlied.
Die Dampfwalze wummert
die zweite
Ilias
ins aufgerissene
Pflaster,

sandgesäumt
staunen die alten
Bilder sich nach, in die Gosse,

ölig verbluten die Krieger
in Silberpfützen, am Straßen-
rand, tuckernd,

Troja, das staubbekrönte,
sieht ein.

SPEECH OF BARRICADING DRUMS, song of drums barricading.
The steamroller rumbles
a second
Iliad
into the torn
pavement,

sand-bordered
the old images
startle themselves in the gutter,

the dying warriors shed blood like oil
in silver puddles, on the road-
side, death-rattle,

Troy, the dust-crowned,
understands.

UNTER DER FLUT
fliegen, an
gehöhten schwarzen
Opfersteinen vorbei,

die unendlich geerdete Schwermut
in den
Fahrwerkschächten,

berauschte Flugschreiber im
Sehnsuchtsgehänge,

künftige Fundstücke, silbrig,
im
schädligen Cockpit,

Sichttunnels, in
den Sprachnebel geblasen,

Selbstzündblumen
an allen Kabeln,

im großen, unausgefahrenen
Felgenring deinen
genabten Schatten,
Saturn.

UNDER THE FLOOD
they fly, past
raised black
sacrificial stones,

the sadness endlessly earth-bound
in the
shafts of landing gear,

drunken air-scribes in
the slopes of longing,

fragments of future findings, silver,
in
the cranial cockpit,

tunnels of vision
blown into the fog of speech,

self-kindling flowers
on every cable,

in the great wheel
not yet worn away,
your shadow, Saturn,
etched deep.

WAHNGÄNGER-AUGEN: in euch
münden die übrigen Blicke.

Eine einzige
Flut
schwillt an.

Bald glänzt ihr
den Felsen zutode, auf den sie
gesetzt
haben, wider
sich selbst.

MAD-FARER'S EYES: all other
gazes flow into you.

A single
flood
swells.

Soon you gleam
the rock to death, upon which
they have
built against
themselves.

MERKBLÄTTER-SCHMERZ,
beschneit, überschneit:

in der Kalenderlücke
wiegt ihn, wiegt ihn
das neugeborene
Nichts.

LEAFLETS-PAIN,
snowed on, snowed over:

in the gap of the calendar
the newborn
Nothing
rocks him, rocks him.

TRECKSCHUTENZEIT,
die Halbverwandelten schleppen
an einer der Welten,

der Enthöhte, geinnigt,
spricht unter den Stirnen am Ufer:

Todes quitt, Gottes
quitt.

Hour of the barge,
the half-transformed bear the load
of one of the worlds,

cast from the throne, he turned inwards,
speaks among brows on the shore:

rid of death, rid
of God.

Schneepart

Snow-Part

WAS NÄHT
an dieser Stimme? Woran
näht diese
Stimme
diesseits, jenseits?

Die Abgründe sind
eingeschworen auf Weiß, ihnen
entstieg
die Schneenadel,

schluck sie,

du ordnest die Welt,
das zählt
soviel wie neun Namen,
auf Knien genannt,

Tumuli, Tumuli,
du
hügelst hinweg, lebendig,
komm
in den Kuß,

ein Flossenschlag,
stet,
lichtet die Buchten,
du gehst
vor Anker, dein Schatten
streift dich ab im Gebüsch,

WHAT SEWS
this voice? On what
does it sew, this
voice
here-and-now, elsewhere?

The abysses are
sworn fast to White, from them
rose
the snow needle,

swallow it,

you order the world,
that counts
as much as nine names
named kneeling,

Tumuli, Tumuli,
you
hurtle away, you the quick,
come
into the kiss,

a fin-beat,
steady,
clears the bays,
you cast
anchor, your shadow
leaves you stranded in the copse,

Ankunft,
Abkunft,

ein Käfer erkennt dich,
ihr steht euch
bevor,
Raupen
spinnen euch ein,

die Große
Kugel
gewährt euch den Durchzug,

bald
knüpft das Blatt seine Ader an deine,
Funken
müssen hindurch,
eine Atemnot lang,

es steht dir ein Baum zu, ein Tag,
er entziffert die Zahl,

ein Wort, mit all seinem Grün,
geht in sich, verpflanzt sich,

folg ihm

arrival,
ancestral,

a beetle recognizes you,
you are about
to happen,
grubs
spin around you,

the Great
Sphere
permits your passage,

soon
the leaf knits its vein to yours,
sparks
must pass through,
for one spell of short breath,

there should be a tree for you, a day,
it deciphers the number,

a word, with all its green,
goes into itself, transplants itself,

follow it

IN ECHSEN-
häute, Fall-
süchtige,
bett ich dich, auf den Simsen,
die Giebel-
löcher
schütten uns zu, mit Lichtdung.

IN SAURIAN
skins, I bed you, you
have the falling sickness, down
on the sills,
the gable-
holes
bury us with the dung of light.

SCHNEEPART, gebäumt, bis zuletzt,
im Aufwind, vor
den für immer entfensterten
Hütten:

Flachträume schirken
übers
geriffelte Eis;

die Wortschatten
heraushaun, sie klaftern
rings um den Krampen
im Kolk.

SNOW-VOICE, reared, to the last,
in the rising wind, before
huts
forever windowless:

flat-dreams cry
across
the rippled ice;

to hew out
word-shadows, to stack them
around the clamps
in the fosse.

SCHLUDERE, Schmerz,
schlag ihr nicht ins Gesicht,
erpfusch dir
die Sandknubbe im
weißen Daneben.

BE CARELESS, pain,
don't strike her in the face,
scheme to get
the sand-knot in
the white Beside.

VON QUERAB
komm ein, als die Nacht,
das Notsegel
bauscht sich,

eingeschreint
an Bord
ist dein Schrei,
du warst da, du bist unten,

unterhalb bist du,

ich geh, ich geh mit den Fingern
von mir,
dich zu sehn,
mit den Fingern, du Untre,

die Armstrünke wuchern,

das Leuchtfeuer denkt
für den ein-
sternigen Himmel,

mit dem Schwertkiel
les ich dich auf.

FROM THE BEAM
come in like the night,
the last sail
billows,

on board
your scream
enshrined,
you were there, you are below,

you are down below,

I go, I go with my
fingers
towards you,
to you down there, with fingers,

the arm-stalks multiply,

the beacon broods
instead of the one-
starred heaven,

with the drop-keel
I get a reading from you.

HOLZGESICHTIGER,
schlackermäuliger
Narr überm Tretrad:

am Ohrlappen hängt
dir das Aug
und hüpft
begrünt.

WOODEN-FACED,
slack-jawed
fool above the treadmill:

on your earlobe hangs
your eye
and skips about
greened over.

MIT DEN SACKGASSEN sprechen
vom Gegenüber,
von seiner
expatriierten
Bedeutung—:

dieses
Brot kauen, mit
Schreibzähnen.

To SPEAK WITH blind alleys
about the face-to-face,
about its
expatriate
meaning—:

to chew
this bread, with
writing teeth.

ETWAS WIE NACHT, scharf-
züngiger als
gestern, als morgen;

etwas wie einer
Fischmäuligen Gruß
übern Jammer-
tresen;

etwas Zusammengewehtes
in Kinderfäusten;

etwas aus meinem
und keinerlei Stoff.

SOMETHING LIKE NIGHT, more sharp-
tongued than
yesterday, than tomorrow;

something like the
fish-wife's greeting
across the counter
of misery;

something blown together
in children's fists;

something from my
nothing-at-all material.

WARUM DIESES JÄHE ZUHAUSE, mittenaus, mittenein?
Ich kann mich, schau, in dich senken, gletschrig,
du selbst erschlägst deine Brüder:
eher als sie
war ich bei dir, Geschneete.

Wirf deine Tropen
zum Rest:
einer will wissen,
warum ich bei Gott
nicht anders war als bei dir,

einer
will drin ersaufen,
zwei Bücher an Stelle der Lungen,

einer, der sich in dich stach,
beatmet den Stich,

einer, er war dir der nächste,
geht sich verloren,

einer schmückt dein Geschlecht
mit deinem und seinem Verrat,

vielleicht
war ich jeder

WHY THIS HASTY HOME, from the midst, in the midst?
See, I can sink myself into you, glacial,
you yourself kill your brothers:
before them
I was with you, snow-sprung-one.

Throw your tropes
to the rest:
someone wants to know,
why I was no different
with God than with you,

someone
wants to drown in it,
two books instead of lungs,

someone, who thrust himself into you,
breathes upon the thrust,

someone, he was closest to you,
loses himself,

someone adorns your sex
with your betrayal and his own,

perhaps
I was everyone

LEVKOJEN, katzenbemündigt.
Beweibt
rechts von dir dieser Rasen.

Stab- und Mondsichel-Patt.

Du sollst nicht, so, gleich dir, hinterm Gitter, damals,
der
maltesische Jude, groß-
lippig——ihn
sprang der Knochen an, jäher
als dich, der Knochen,
den ein schon Morgiger warf—,
du
sollst nicht
aufsehn zum Himmel, du ließest
ihn denn, wie er dich,
im Stich, neben-
lichtig.
. . . .
Schwester Kastanie, Vielblatt,
mit deinem blanken
Hiedrüben.

GILLYFLOWERS, cat-mouthed.
With woman,
this meadow at your right.

Staff and crescent moon-checkmate.

Thus, thou shalt not, like you then, behind the grid,
the
Jew of Malta, thick-
lipped—the
bone leapt at him, more sudden
than you, the bone,
thrown by someone already tomorrow's—
thou
shalt not
look up into the sky, unless you left
it, as it did you,
in the lurch, side-
lit.
. . . .
Sister chestnut, many-leafed,
with your shining
Here-sidedness.

FÜR ERIC

In der Flüstertüte
buddelt Geschichte,

in den Vororten raupen die Tanks,

unser Glas
füllt sich mit Seide,

wir stehn.

FOR ERIC

In the megaphone
history is grubbing away,

in the suburbs tanks creep like caterpillars,

our glass
fills itself with silk,

we stand.

DEIN BLONDSCHATTEN, auf
Schwimmtrense gezäumt,
schwenkt die Wasserschabracke,

—auch du
hättest ein Recht auf Paris,
würdest du deiner
bitterer inne—,

dein Hankenmal, farblos
skizziert es die halb-
nahe Levade.

YOUR BLOND SHADOW, hitched
to the swimming lead,
shakes the water gear,

—you, too
would have a right to Paris,
if yours were a more
bitter self-knowledge—,

the mark on your flank, colorless
sketches the com-
ing levade.

DIE ABGRÜNDE STREUNEN: Summkies——:

dem kommst du bei
mit Taubheitsgefühlen
und Unschlaf,

und kämen——die Lockstoffe geistern
den Fahnenmast hoch——,
kämen auch hier
die Albembleme geflattert,
du wärst, dich erplündernd,
gebieterisch-gleich
ihr Entzwei.

THE ABYSSES ARE STRAYING: Humming scree—:

you take care of that
with numbness of feeling
and non-sleep,

and if—allurements are haunting
the heights of the flagpole—,
and if even here
the incubus-signs were sent fluttering,
you would, plundering yourself,
as if in defiance
be their sundering.

DEIN MÄHNEN-ECHO
—ihm wusch ich den Stein aus—,
mit Rauhreif beschlagen,
mit entsiegelter
Stirn beleu-
mundet
von mir.

THE ECHO OF YOUR MANE
—I washed the stone from it—,
coated with hoarfrost,
to the un-
sealing
of your forehead
I stand witness.

DER HALBZERFRESSENE Wimpel
frißt alle Länder vom Meer fort,
alle Meere vom Land,

ein weiterer Name
—du, du beleb dich!—
muß eine Ziffer
dulden,

Unzählbarer du:
um ein Un-
zeichen
bist du ihnen allen
voraus.

THE HALF-DEVOURED pennant
devours all lands from the sea,
all seas from the land,

another name
—you, you come to live!—
must endure
a number,

you, never-to-be-counted:
by one null-
token
you are ahead of
them all.

Aus der Vergängnis
stehen die Stufen,

das ins Ohr Geträufelte
mündigt die Vorzeit darin,

Fjorde
sind Dochte,

nüchtern Erzähltes
träumt,

du berührst es, ein Tag-
verschworner.

OUT OF DECAY
rise the steps,

what has been trickled into the ear
makes the past come of age,

fjords
are wicks,

the prosy tale
is dreaming,

you touch it, you the day-
sworn.

AUS DEM MOORBODEN ins
Ohnebild steigen,
ein Häm
im Flintenlauf Hoffnung,
das Ziel, wie Ungeduld mündig,
darin.

Dorfluft, rue Tournefort.

To CLIMB from marshy soil
into non-image
is blood
in the gun-barrel hope,
the target, is within
like impatience come of age.

Country air, rue Tournefort.

LÖSSPUPPEN: also
hier steints nicht,

nur Landschneckenhäuser,
unausgeblasen,
sagen zur Wüste: du
bist bevölkert—:

die Wildpferde stoßen
in Mammut-
hörner:

Petrarca
ist wieder
in Sicht.

LOESS-CHRYSALIDS: so
no stones stake it out here,

only snail shells
unblown,
tell the desert: you
are populated——:

the wild horses blow
Mammoth-
trumpets:

Petrarch
is again
in sight.

MITERHOBEN
von den Geräuschen,
forderst du—Glas
feindet an, was immer
undurchdringlicher dein ist—,
forderst du alles
in seine Aura,

das Quentchen Mut
bittert sich ein,
wachsam:
es weiß, daß du weißt.

EXALTED
by the clamor
you summon—glass
makes enemies, whatever
is more and more impenetrably yours—,
you summon everything
into its aura,

the small dram of courage
becomes bitter,
watchful:
It knows that you know.

STEINSCHLAG hinter den Käfern.
Da sah ich einen, der log nicht,
heimstehn in seine Verzweiflung.

Wie deinem Einsamkeitssturm
glückt ihm die weit
ausschreitende Stille.

HAIL OF STONES behind the beetles.
There I saw one, he did not lie,
stand fast in his despair.

Like your storm of solitude
he succeeds
in far-striding silence.

ICH SCHREITE deinen Verrat aus,
Fußspangen an
allen Seins-
gelenken,

Krümelgeister
kalben
aus deinen gläsernen
Titten,

mein Stein ist gekommen zu dir,
selbstentgittert, du inwendig
Ottern-
befrachtete,

du verhebst dich
an meinem leichtesten Schmerz,

du wirst sichtbar,

irgendein Toter, ganz bei sich,
setzt Lee über Luv.

MY STRIDE takes the measure of your betrayal,
shackled on
every limb
of being,

hobgoblins
calve
from your glassy
tits,

my stone is upon you,
self-un-latticed, you are
teeming with vipers
within,

you over-strain yourself
at my slightest pain,

you become visible,

some dead man, all by himself,
sets course against the wind.

KALK-KROKUS, im
Hellwerden: dein
steckbriefgereiftes
Von-dort-und-auch-dort-her,
unspaltbar,

Sprengstoffe
lächeln dir zu,
die Delle Dasein
hilft einer Flocke
aus sich heraus,

in den Fundgruben
staut sich die Moldau.

CHALK-CROCUS, at
the coming of light: your
indivisible
mellowed in the warrant,
From-here-and-there-too,

high explosives
are smiling at you,
existence the nick
helps a snowflake
come out of itself,

at the source-points
the Moldau is rising.

HINTER SCHLÄFENSPLITTERN,
im notfrischen
Holzwein,

(der Ort, wo du herkommst,
er redet sich finster, südwärts),

dahlienfürchtig bei Gold,
auf immer heiterern
Stühlen.

BEHIND SPLINTERS OF SKULL,
in wood-wine
fresh with need,

(the place where you come from
talks itself into darkness, southward),

fearful of dahlias in their gold,
on chairs evermore
serene.

DAS GEDUNKELTE Splitterecho,
hirnstrom-
hin,

die Buhne über der Windung,
auf die es zu stehn kommt,

soviel
Unverfenstertes dort,
sieh nur,

die Schütte
müßiger Andacht,
einen
Kolbenschlag von
den Gebetssilos weg,

einen und keinen.

THE DARKENED splinter-echo
brain-stream
tide,

the jetty above the bend
where it comes to stand,

just look
so much un-windowed
over there,

the heap
of idle devotion,
one
stroke of the piston
away from prayer-siloes,

one and none.

Zeitgehöft

Farmstead of Time

VON DER SINKENDEN WALSTIRN
les ich dich ab—
du erkennst mich,

der Himmel
stürzt sich
in die Harpune,

sechsbeinig
hockt unser Stern im Schaum,

langsam
hißt einer, der's sieht,
den Trosthappen: das
balzende Nichts.

FROM THE SINKING WHALEBROW
I read you—
you recognize me,

heaven
hurls itself
into the harpoon,

six-legged
our star crouches in the foam,

slowly
someone who sees it hoists
a scrap of comfort: the
strutting Nothingness.

DU LIEGST HINAUS
über dich,

über dich hinaus
liegt dein Schicksal,

weißäugig, einem Gesang
entronnen, tritt etwas zu ihm,
das hilft
beim Zungenentwurzeln,
auch mittags, draußen.

YOU LIE BEYOND
yourself,

beyond yourself
lies your fate,

white-eyed, it has fled
from a song, something comes forth,
it's useful
in the tearing of tongues from their roots,
even in the afternoon, out there.

Die Weinbergsmauer erstürmt
vom Ewigkeitsklirren,
die Reben
meutern,

miterklirrt
das Rückenmark, bei
Herzschwüle, im
wirklicheren Gehäus,

die fünf Körner verteilt
auf die vier Meere,

tauch ein.

The vineyard wall stormed
by the clatter of eternity,
the vines
mutiny,

the spinal cord
clatters too, in the
heart's unease, in
the truer housing,

the five grains are divided
among the four seas,

dive in.

EINGESCHOSSEN
in die Smaragdbahn,

Larvenschlupf, Sternschlupf, mit allen
Kielen
such ich dich,
Ungrund.

SHOT FORTH
in the emerald race,

hatching of grubs, hatching of stars, with every
keel
I search for you,
Fathomless.

VOR MEIN
wetterleuchtendes Knie
kommt die Hand zu stehn,
mit der du
dir übers Aug fuhrst,

ein Klirren
holt sich Gewißheit
im Kreis, den ich zog
um uns zwei,

manchmal freilich
stirbt der Himmel
unsern Scherben
voraus.

IN FRONT OF MY
summer-lightning-knee
the hand
you brushed over your eye
comes to halt,

a clatter
draws certainty
from the circle I drew
around the two of us,

sometimes, however,
the sky dies
ahead of
our shards.

Du wirfst mir Ertrinkendem
Gold nach:
vielleicht läßt ein Fisch
sich bestechen.

YOU ARE THROWING gold after me
I am drowning:
perhaps a fish can be
bribed.

AN DIE HALTLOSIGKEITEN
sich schmiegen:

es schnippen
zwei Finger im Abgrund, in den
Sudelheften
rauscht Welt auf, es kommt
auf dich an.

To CLING
to unstable things:

two fingers are snapping
in the abyss, a
world is stirring
in the scratch-sheets, it all depends
on you.

DEIN UHRENGESICHT,
von Blaufeuern über-
lagert,
verschenkt seine Ziffern,

meine
Herkunft
hielt Umschau, sie geht
in dich ein, die mit-
vereinten
Kristalle
flennen.

YOUR CLOCK-FACE,
by blue fires over-
laid,
gives away its numbers,

my
descent
took a long look, it enters
you, the com-
pacted
crystals
are weeping.

ICH LOTSE DICH hinter die Welt,
da bist du bei dir, unbeirrbar,
heiter

vermessen die Stare den Tod,
das Schilf winkt dem Stein ab, du hast
alles

für heut abend.

I PILOT YOU behind the world,
there you are with yourself, unflinching,
serene
the starlings take a survey of death,
the reeds sign a warning to stone, you have
everything
for this evening.

MEINE
dir zugewinkelte Seele
hört dich
gewittern,

in deiner Halsgrube lernt
mein Stern, wie man wegsackt
und wahr wird,

ich fingre ihn wieder heraus—
komm, besprich dich mit ihm,
noch heute.

My
soul, inclined towards you
hears you
thundering,

in the pit of your throat
my star learns to sink
and become true,

I pull it out again—
come, conjure with it,
this very day.

MANDELNDE, die du nur halbsprachst,
doch durchzittert vom Keim her,
dich
ließ ich warten,
dich.

Und war
noch nicht
entäugt,
noch unverdornt im Gestirn
des Lieds, das beginnt:
Hachnissini.

ALMOND-LIKE, you who only halfspoke,
still shaken from the bud,
you
I left waiting,
you.

And was
not yet
made eyeless
not yet thorn-covered in the star-group
of the song beginning:
Hachnissini.

ES STAND
der Feigensplitter auf deiner Lippe,

es stand
Jerusalem um uns,

es stand
der Hellkiefernduft
überm Dänenschiff, dem wir dankten,

ich stand
in dir.

THERE WAS
the fig-splinter on your lip,

there was
Jerusalem around us,

there was
the fragrance of blond pine
above the Danish ship, we were grateful for it,

there was I
within you.

WIR, DIE WIE DER STRANDHAFER WAHREN,
in N'we Awiwim,

der ungeküßte
Stein einer Klage
rauscht auf,
vor Erfüllung,

er befühlt unsre Münder,
er wechselt
über zu uns,

eingetan ist uns
sein Weiß,

wir geben uns weiter:
an dich und an mich,

die Nacht, sieh dich vor, die sand-
befehligte,
nimmt es genau
mit uns zwein.

WE, WHO WERE TRUE LIKE THE BENT GRASS,
in N'we Awiwim,

the unkissed
stone of grief
is stirring
in fulfillment,

it handles our mouths,
it changes
over to us,

its White is become one
with us,

we hand ourselves on:
to you and to me,

watch out, the night, the sand-
commandeered,
is painstaking
with the two of us.

EIN RING, ZUM BOGENSPANNEN,
nachgeschickt einem Wortschwarm,
der wegstürzt hinter die Welt,
mit den Staren,

Pfeilige, wenn du mir zuschwirrst,
weiß ich, woher,

vergeß ich, woher.

A RING, FOR DRAWING THE BOW,
sent after a swarm of words,
it plunges behind the world
with the starlings,

when, like an arrow, you whir towards me,
I know, wherefrom,

I forget, wherefrom.

Komm, leg die Welt aus mit dir,
komm, laß mich euch zuschütten mit
allem Meinen,

Eins mit dir bin ich,
uns zu erbeuten,

auch jetzt.

COME, cover the world with yourself,
come, let me bury you all with
everything of my own,

I am one with you,
to capture us,

even now.

EINEN STIEFELVOLL Hirn
in den Regen gestellt:

es wird ein Gehn sein, ein großes,
weit über die Grenzen,
die sie uns ziehn.

A BOOT FULL of brain
kicked out in the rain:

there will be a return, a great one,
far beyond the borders,
they draw for us.

ICH TRINK WEIN aus zwei Gläsern
und zackere an
der Königszäsur
wie Jener
am Pindar,

Gott gibt die Stimmgabel ab
als einer der kleinen
Gerechten,

aus der Lostrommel fällt
unser Deut.

I DRINK WINE from two glasses
and comb through
the king's cæsura
like that one
with Pindar,

God turns over the tuning-fork
alone of the small
just ones,

from the fate-engine falls
our measure.

Es WIRD etwas sein, später,
das füllt sich mit dir
und hebt sich
an einen Mund

Aus dem zerscherbten
Wahn
steh ich auf
und seh meiner Hand zu,
wie sie den einen
einzigen
Kreis zieht

THERE WILL BE something, later,
which fills itself with you
and heaves itself
unto a mouth

From the fragmented
madness
I get up
and watch my hand,
as it sketches the
single
circle

WIE ICH den Ringschatten trage,
trägst du den Ring,

etwas, das Schweres gewohnt ist,
verhebt sich
an uns,
unendlich
Entimmernde du.

As I bear the ring's shadow,
you bear the ring,

something used to burdens
strains
lifting us,
you endlessly
making an end of things.

DAS FREMDE
hat uns im Netz,
die Vergänglichkeit greift
ratlos durch uns hindurch,

zähl meinen Puls, auch ihn,
in dich hinein,

dann kommen wir auf,
gegen dich, gegen mich,

etwas kleidet uns ein,
in Taghaut, in Nachthaut,
fürs Spiel mit dem obersten, fall-
süchtigen Ernst.

FOREIGN THINGS
ensnare us,
transiency helpless
grasps us through and through,

take my pulse, even that,
unto yourself,

then we succeed
against you, against me,

something dresses us up
in day-hide, in night-hide
for the game of the highest gravity
of fallingsickness.

UMLICHTET die Keime,
die ich in dir
erschwamm,

freigerudert
die Namen—sie
befahren die Engen,

ein Segensspruch, vorn,
ballt sich
zur wetterfühligen
Faust.

THE SPORES surrounded by light,
which I reached
by swimming inside you,

the names
rowed free—they
sail the straits,

a benediction, in front,
curls
into a fist for
feeling the weather.

ORTSWECHSEL bei den Substanzen:
geh du zu dir, schließ dich an,
bei verschollenem
Erdlicht,

ich höre, wir waren
ein Himmelsgewächs,
das bleibt zu beweisen, von
obenher, an
unsern Wurzeln entlang,

zwei Sonnen gibts, hörst du,
zwei,
nicht eine—
ja und?

RELOCATION among the substances:
go to yourself, take part
where earthlight
is missing,

I hear we were
a shoot of heaven,
that remains to be revealed, from
above, along
our roots,

there are two suns, do you hear,
two,
not one—
so what?

DIE GESENKTEN
Götterdaumen, ich hole, im Borken-
hemd,
die untersten Baumläufer ein, bald ist
heute, für immer, die
Markierungen, das
Strahlengezücht,
kommen
über die Antimaterie
getanzt, zu dir,
in die Kometen-
Schonung.

THE THUMBS of the gods
turned down, I in my bark-
shirt
catch up with the lowest tree-creepers, soon
it's today forever, the
markings, this
brood of rays,
they come
dancing, to you
across anti-matter
into the nursery
of comets.

KROKUS, vom gastlichen
Tisch aus gesehn:
zeichenfühliges
kleines Exil
einer gemeinsamen
Wahrheit,
du brauchst
jeden Halm.

CROCUS, seen from
the hospitable table:
sign-conscious
little exile
of a mutual
truth,
you need
every blade.

REBLEUTE graben
die dunkelstündige Uhr um,
Tiefe um Tiefe,

du liest,

es fordert
der Unsichtbare den Wind
in die Schranken,

du liest,

die Offenen tragen
den Stein hinterm Aug,
der erkennt dich,
am Sabbath.

GRAPEGROWERS dig
for the dark-houred clock
depth by depth,

you read,

the invisible one
he orders the winds
behind their borders,

you read,

the open ones carry
the stone behind their eye,
it recognizes you
on the Sabbath.

CONVERSATION
IN THE MOUNTAINS

Paul Celan wrote "Conversation in the Mountains" in August, 1959, shortly after a missed meeting with an unnamed person on a mountain road. What he wrote after that failed rendezvous was a language-parable, mimicking the nineteenth-century Romantic quest in which the ascent of mountains becomes a striving for the union of the soul with nature. The landscape of Celan's piece recalls the Alpine terrain of stone, fields, and fir-trees which Büchner's Lenz crosses in the 1837 fragment, but instead of the clamorous daylight of Lenz we have a world grown dark and silent, where "things have gone down in the west." This is also the landscape of folktale, where plants, flowers, and stones may or may not speak to the traveller, where to travel without one's own shadow is to travel in search of a soul.

There are echoes of at least three different dialogues in Celan's story. We hear Büchner's address to Lenz, the artist at the end of his tether, "burrowing into the universe," but finding himself "in the void." Lenz, too, tries to talk to himself, but cannot, his sentences trailing off into echolalia, madness, and silence.

Büchner to Lenz: Celan to Osip Mandelstam, his older "cousin" and predecessor, who struggled himself with silence and extinction. Mandelstam, like Celan, was preoccupied with finding a language for the "here and now," a language where green, the color of time, of both growth and decay, might meet with white, the color of the absolute, the pure, eternal, unchanging word. (In Mandelstam's memoir-fable, The Noise of Time, he refers to the Jews of St. Petersburg, dispossessed of their own language, as "tongue-tied," as "babblers.")

Celan to Celan: Celan, the German poet, writing in cultural exile in Paris, addresses Celan the Jew. Celan the Jew is a survivor, writing in a language "borrowed not lent," the language of the other, conversing over his shoulder with No One, his "Do you hear" answered by an echo. But in this dialogue between the opposing selves, there is a progression, beginning with an inarticulate stammer, then proceeding through paradox, indirection, and the evocation of images from Celan's poetic lexicon: stone, star, veil, thread, and Sabbath candle—to fluency. The act of writing poetry, that is, in Celan's bleak metaphor, the stutter of a blindman's stick on stone, is nonetheless a redemptive solution to the language riddle, a way up, a way into the self.   K.W.

One evening, after the sun (and not only the sun) had gone down in the west, the Jew went for a walk, that is to say he stepped out of his hut and went for a walk, the Jew, the son of a Jew, and his name went with him, his unspeakable name, as he walked and went on and went shuffling along, you could hear it, going with stick, going on stone, now can you hear me, hear me you shall, here am I, I, I and that one whom you hear, whom you just think you hear, I and the other—he walked and made himself heard, walked out one evening when all sorts of things had gone down in the west, went on under the cloudmass, went on in shadow, his own and the other's— for the Jew, you know, what does he have that he really owns that's neither borrowed nor lent and never returned—and there he walked and went on his way, went along the road, the beautiful road, the incomparable road, he went on like Lenz through the mountains, he to whom it was granted to live down there in the lowlands where he belongs, he went on and on.

Ah yes, he went on down the road, the beautiful road.

And who do you think came towards him? His cousin, his cousin, his own first cousin came towards him, he was older by a quarter of a Jew's lifetime, he was tall, he came towards him, he went on, he too in shadow, that which was borrowed—for who, I ask and ask once more, when God has made him a Jew, comes along with his very own things?—he came, he was tall, he came towards the other, Tall came to Small, the Jew bid his stick be still before the stick of Jew Tall.

Even stone too was still, and there was a stillness in the mountains where they went, he and the other.

So it was silent indeed, it was silent up there in the mountains. Not silent for long, for if a Jew comes along and encounters another one, then silence is soon done for, even in the mountains. For a Jew and nature, those are once and for all two quite different things, even here, even now.

And so there they stand, the first cousins, and on the left the Turk's-cap lily is growing, it grows wild, it grows as it does nowhere else, and there on the right, there's Lamb's Lettuce and *Dianthus superbus*, the gillyflower, is not far away. But they, the first cousins, they have (it cries out to heaven) no eyes. As a matter of fact, they have eyes, even they, but there's a veil before them, not in front, no, but in back, a detachable veil: an image barely enters before it gets caught in the web and soon there's a thread which winds itself and entwines itself around the image, a thread from the veil; it winds itself around the image and gets it with child, half-image, half-veil.

Poor Turk's-cap, poor Lamb's Lettuce. There they stand, the first cousins, they stand on a road in the mountains, silent stick and silent stone, the silence no silence at all, no word has grown dumb here, no sentence, it's just a pause, just a hiatus, an empty space, you can see the syllables standing around; they're tongue and mouth, those two, as they were before, and there's a veil on their eyes, and you, you poor things, you neither stand there nor do you bloom, you don't exist. July is not July is not July.

Those babblers! Even now, tongues tied and lips sealed tight, they have something to say! Well, let them talk . . .

"You came from far away, came here . . ."

"So I did. I came. I came, like you."

"I know that."

"You do know. You know what you see: The earth has folded up here, folded over once, then twice, then three times, and split open in the middle, and in the middle there is water, the water is green, the Green is white and the White comes from still further on high, comes from the glaciers, one could say, but shouldn't, that this is a language for the here and now, the Green with the White within, a language for neither you nor me—for I ask, for whom is it meant, this earth, for

I say it is not meant for you or for me—a language, to be sure, without I or Thou, merely He, merely It, do you understand, merely She and nothing more."

"I understand, I do understand. Because I came, ah yes, from afar, ah yes, I came like you."

"I know."

"You know and you want to ask me: And nonetheless you came, nonetheless you came up here—why, and whatever for?"

"Why and whatever for . . . Perhaps because I had to talk to myself or to you, because I had to talk with mouth and tongue, not only with stick. For to whom does he talk, the stick? He talks to stone, and the stone—to whom does he talk?"

"To whom should he talk, cousin? He doesn't talk, he speaks, and he who speaks, cousin, talks to no one, he speaks because no one hears him, no one and No One and then he, he says, not his mouth or his tongue, he says, and not only he: Do you hear?"

"Do you hear, he says—I know, first cousin, I know . . . Do you hear, he says, here I am, I am, I am here, I have come. Come with the stick, I and no other, I and not he, I with my hour, appointed not deserved, I who was dealt the blow, I who was not, I with my memory, I, with memory failing, I, I, I . . ."

"He says, he says . . . Do you hear, he says . . . And D'y'hear, surely, D'y'hear, he says nothing, he doesn't answer, for D'y'hear, that is the one with the glaciers, the one folded over threefold, but not for mankind . . . The Green-

and-White over there, the one with the Turk's-cap, the one
with the Lamb's Lettuce . . . But I, cousin, I who just stand,
here on this road, here where I don't belong, today, now,
since it's gone down in the west, it and its light, I here with
the shadow, my own and the other's, I—I who can tell you:

"—I was lying on the stone then, you know, on the flag-
stones; and they lay next to me, the others who were like me,
the others who were different from me and the same, those
first cousins; and they lay there and slept, they slept and slept
not, and they dreamt and dreamt not, and they did not love
me and I loved them not, for I was one and who would love
one, and there were many more still than lay around me, and
who'd wish to be able to love all, and I, I will not keep this
from you, I did not love them, those who could not love me, I
loved the burning candle there on the left in the corner, I
loved it because it burned down, not because *it* burned down,
for *it* was *his* candle, the candle that he, the father of our
mothers had lit, because that evening a day began, a singular
one, a day, the seventh day, the seventh upon which the first
was bound to follow, the seventh and not the last one, I loved,
cousin, not it, I loved its burning down, and do you know, I
have not loved anything since;

"no, nothing: or perhaps that which burned down like that
candle on that day, on the seventh and not the last; not the
last, no, for yes, I am here on this road, they say it's beautiful,
yes I am, next to the Turk's-cap and the Lamb's Lettuce, and
a hundred steps away, over there, within reach, there the larch
tree grows right up to the stone-pine, I see it, I see it and
don't, and my stick, it spoke to stone, and my stick is silent

now, and the stone, it can speak, you say, and in my eyes there's the veil, the detachable one, there are veils, detachable veils, and when you've lifted one, there's a second one too and the star—for now it stands above the mountains—if it wants to come in, it will have to be married, and soon it will no longer be itself, but half-veil and half-star, and I know, I know, cousin, I know, I met you here and we talked a great deal, and the folds there, you know, they exist neither for mankind nor for us, who walked and met each other, for us here under the star, for us, the Jews who came like Lenz through the mountains, Thou Tall and I Small, you a babbler and I a babbler, we with our sticks, we with our names, unspeakable names, we with our shadows, our own and the other's, here are you and here am I—

"I here, I: I who can tell you all, who could have told you; I who will not tell you and have not told you: I with the Turk's-cap to the left, I with the Lamb's Lettuce, I with the burned-down thing, with the candle, I with the day, I with the days, I now here and I now there, I perhaps accompanied—at last! —by the love of those unloved, I on the way to myself, up here."